SALUTATION TO THE SUN

SALUTATION TO THE SUN

A DAILY EXERCISE FOR A VITAL LIFE

Rita Beintema

Translated from the Dutch by Jill Penton

Saffron Walden
The C.W. Daniel Company Limited

First published in the Netherlands by
Uitgeverj Ankh-Hermes bv, Deventer

This English translation first published in Great Britain by
The C. W. Daniel Company Limited
1 Church Path, Saffron Walden, Essex, CB10 1JP,
England

ISBN 0 85207 304 6

The photographs throughout the text by Henk Eilander, with grateful
thanks to Jos Horst.

Produced in association with
Book Production Consultants plc
25–27 High Street, Chesterton, Cambridge CB4 1ND

Printed and bound by Hillman Printers (Frome) Ltd

CONTENTS

THE CANTICLE OF

BROTHER SUN

Exalted, almighty, good Lord,
You are the praise, the glory and the honour
and all blessings.
To you alone they come, Almighty, and no man
is worthy to call you.

Praise be, my Lord, with all your creations,
especially Lord Brother Sun,
who brings the gift of daylight and through
whom God lets everything be seen.
And he is beautiful and shines with great splen-
dour: he is a sign, Almighty, of You.

Praise be, my Lord, through sister Moon and
the Stars.
You placed them in the heavens, clear, precious
and charming.

Praise be, my Lord, through brother Wind and
through the air and the clouds, through the
clear and all other weather: through them
You maintain your creations.

Praise be, my Lord, through sister Water who is
so useful and meek, so splendid and pure.

Praise be, my Lord, through brother Fire who
    brings us your light in the night.
He is so sweet and cheerful and unyielding in
    his power.

Praise be, my Lord, through our sister mother
    Earth who carries and feeds us and grows all
    sorts of plants, colourful flowers and grass.

Praise be, my Lord, through the People, who
    out of love grant You forgiveness and bear
    sickness and difficulty.
Happy are those who keep the peace, as they
    shall be crowned by You, Almighty.

Praise and blessing, my Lord, thank Him and
    serve Him, with great humbleness.

Francis of Assisi (1182-1226)

INTRODUCTION

The salutation to the sun probably originates from India, from the vedic time, although the exact date remains unknown. The sun is, however, mentioned in the oldest manuscript from that time, in one of the holy books: the Rig Veda (approximately 3000 to 6000 years B.C.) In this Rig Veda ten hymns (songs) are dedicated to the sun.

It was not unusual for people to worship the sun or the creator of the sun. This form of worship was common in many cultures, including those in Egypt, Persia and Greece.

Plato also wrote about sun worship; he considered the sun to be the symbol of goodness. Many centuries later in his 'Psalm praising Creation', Francis of Assisi also makes reference to Lord Brother Sun, who brings the gift of daylight.

Even today the Sioux Indians still say a spoken or silent sun prayer. When praying to the Great Spirit the Indians stand motionless with their arms raised upwards, in the morning facing the rising sun and in the evening facing the setting sun. In 1956 this prayer was said in 134 countries on World Prayer Day.

Even now the sun continues to be the 'creator' of light and life.

In ancient India physical worship of the sun was often practised in the ashrams. These are spiritual communities in which meditation and philosophy are and were practised. In certain ashrams much attention was given to yoga exercises, breathing techniques and body control. It seems probable that the Sun Salutation is derived from several of these yoga positions.

The physical value of the Sun Salutation is considerable. It is performed daily by numerous people all over the world in order to keep their bodies supple, healthy and flexible.

In this booklet you will find the Sun Salutation as I have been teaching it to my students for more than thirty years. There is also a simple, and still effective, version for those people who are stiff in the pelvic region, and thus need more time before being able to perform the real version. I have included a number of preparatory exercises for those who are very stiff. These are intended to make certain body areas, such as the toes, legs, shoulders, arms, wrists and fingers more supple and stronger, so that they can function optimally during the performance of the Sun Salutation. Only then will the Sun Salutation be effective in bringing and maintaining your body up to an optimal condition.

Consult your family doctor if you have (serious) physical complaints. He/she can advise you whether you should or should not perform the Sun Salutation.

Furthermore, you alone are responsible for exceeding your physical ability. Force nothing; for the body will only resist. Patience and attention are the way forward.

I wish you much success.

Rita Beintema

THE THERAPEUTIC EFFECT OF THE SUN SALUTATION

The Sun Salutation consists of several movements which blend together to form a sequence which, after a little practise, everybody is able to perform. Younger people should have little or no problem with the exercise. However as we get older our bodies become stiffer and less flexible, and it will take us slightly more time and effort to perform the Sun Salutation smoothly and well.

The Sun Salutation affects every part of the body. The nervous system, the circulation and the respiration are also significantly influenced.

The spine is bent and stretched during each sequence. In this way the spine regains its flexibility and the muscles are better able to bring or hold the vertebrae in position.

The back and the front of the pelvis is stretched, extended and relaxed. After a time it regains its flexibility which can help prevent osteoarthritis of the pelvis and hips.

The legs, thus also the knees, ankles, and foot joints, become suppler and also stronger because the alternating contraction and relaxation in the movement strengthens the muscles.

The chest, with the ribs, is exercised intensively when the arms are stretched up and lowered down again. This movement has a positive effect on the lungs, the heart and, due to the improved respiration, the psyche too.

Considerably more happens in the abdominal cavity where the stomach, pancreas, liver and gall bladder are to be found. The kidneys and adrenal glands lie somewhat posteriorly; the bladder and uterus lie lower in the abdomen. With every sequence of the Sun Salutation the abdominal contents are massaged and stretched which improves the blood circulation. One ought not to forget or underestimate the effect on the bowels. These are stimulated, so that the abdominal contents do not remain too long in one place and the waste products are removed. Bowels that function well maintain health.

The shoulder and neck muscles are often under considerable strain; which makes them painful and hard. As a result of the movements of the Sun Salutation and the improved respiration, the muscles become much more supple and also stronger. Also the muscle attachments on the head (often a cause of headache) become less inflexible, due to the improved circulation which occurs when the head hangs down during the exercise. The brain also benefits from this improved circulation.

The muscles in the arms and those related to the elbows, wrists and fingers become more supple and stronger.

After a while a correction slowly but surely appears in the body: rounded shoulders and bent backs disappear, hollow backs become less hollow and the head becomes more upright on the trunk.

ENERGY FLOW DURING THE SUN SALUTATION

The concepts of acupuncture and meridians or energy lines have slowly become more familiar whether we want to accept them or not.

In the teachings of acupuncture, energy is known to have a circulation which follows channels, just like the blood circulation. These channels are known as meridians; they are situated on both sides of the body and form a dense network that runs throughout the whole body.

There are twelve principal meridian pairs, situated on the right and left surface of the body; one for each organ system. There are also two midline channels, one running along the front of the body, known as the conception channel, and another running along the back of the body, known as the governor channel. As stated before, meridians are channels for the flow of energy and are connected to specific organs and organ systems. The energy flows through the meridians as a sort of wave, so that each of the twelve pairs receives maximum energy for two out of every twenty-four hours.

The energy in the body is constantly moving; it circulates within a closed system and moves from yin (female energy) to yang (male energy) and from yang to yin in a fluid equilibrium between the two energy poles.

A thing is never completely yang or yin. Where one ceases to exist, the other is already present. The rhythmic movement from yin to yang and from yang to yin is an expression of life itself.

Harmony arises from the balance between yang and yin.

The word acupuncture comes from the words

acus (needle) and punctura (prick). The needle is pricked into one or more points on the meridians in order to restore the balance between yang and yin. In acupuncture everything is seen to be in relationship with everything else; nothing exists on its own. To give an example: disturbance in the large or small intestine can lead to shoulder complaints. Knee conditions may be related to disturbed kidney energy. There are a number of points which, due to stagnation, can cause complaints elsewhere in the body. A doctor is usually unable to find anything wrong at the site and x-rays reveal nothing. Nevertheless the complaint remains and we are left to do something about it ourselves, fortunately this is possible with the appropriate movements and correct breathing.

It is of course possible to influence the whole energy system without using needles. I use knowledge of the meridians as a basis for good movement, breathing and massage.

The energy system is activated and harmonized in the Sun Salutation by the movements which blend and flow into each other, and by the stretch and pressure on different points of the body. Certain body areas are of particular importance in this:

1. the feet
2. the ankles
3. the knees
4. the pelvis
5. the midriff
6. the shoulders
7. all the vertebrae
8. the elbows

9. the wrists
10. the hands

Pain is quick to appear if energy stagnates in these areas. Blocked energy often reveals itself as muscle or joint pain; these painful areas feel better after movement, massage or a warm shower. We are often inclined to move very little and very carefully when we have muscle pain and tend to avoid touching the area; at the very most we might cautiously rub in a muscle liniment. Every sportsman or woman knows however that waste products are removed faster from the muscles with proper movement and breathing and that a good massage can increase this effect. Many people do not know this however, and do neither one nor the other. The result: the blocked energy remains and, often after some time, does or does not get better on its own.

We are of course largely responsible for our own health. With a little effort we are able to deal with a number of complaints ourselves and can thus help the body to function better. Improved movement and better breathing gets the stagnated energy moving, activates the circulation, and increases the removal of waste products and the supply of oxygen-rich blood.

As I have already mentioned, total energy is a twenty-four hour service. The energy increases from 00.00 hours and reaches its maximum at 12.00 hours. The total energy then slowly decreases until midnight. For this reason, and in order to profit from the maximal effect, it is recommended that the Sun Salutation or the exercises are performed in the morning.

BREATHING

The effect of the Sun Salutation is largely due to the flowing movements, whilst the breathing sustains and strengthens the effect. If you do not already have a good technique, it will be very difficult to practise good breathing during the performance of the Sun Salutation. By breathing incorrectly, we puff ourselves up and hold the breath in the wrong way. There is then a danger that we will produce stress rather than health with the Sun Salutation. Correct breathing ensures that oxygen rich blood reaches every cell in the body, so that the body can recover, renew and unburden itself. The movement of respiration corresponds naturally with the physical movement of the Sun Salutation.

PRACTISING ABDOMINAL BREATHING

A good time to practise abdominal breathing is in the morning whilst your stomach is still empty. Go to the toilet first; it is unpleasant to practise with a full bladder and full intestines. Open the bedroom window wide and then lie relaxed on the bed (perhaps under the blankets).

- Rest your hands on your navel.
- Breathe in and out a couple of times and try to observe how you breathe in and breathe out.
- Now try to actively pull in your abdominal muscles, while breathing out through your mouth.
- Abruptly release your abdominal muscles

and allow the air to flow in through your nose. Do not take an active breath, just allow the breath to enter in a relaxed manner. Do not allow the inward flow through your nose to go on for too long: 3 to 5 seconds is sufficient.

- Pull your abdominal muscle in again, while breathing out through your mouth.

Repeat this a few times; stop if you become dizzy. Then try it again. Sometimes you might have the feeling that you are tensing your back muscles instead of your abdominal muscles. Relax for a while and concentrate on your abdominal muscles. After a few days you will develop more feeling for, and control over, pulling in your abdominal muscles actively. You might even have sore muscles for a few of days, but this will disappear before too long.

When you can do this well, you should progress it further. Learn to pull your whole abdomen in slowly; not only under the navel but also just above the pubic arch and between the navel and the subcostal angle. In this way all the abdominal contents are given an extra massage.

- Begin by pulling in your abdomen just above the pubic arch, move onto the navel and then onto the subcostal angle. This a wave like sort of movement. Continue to breathe out whilst pulling the abdominal muscle in.
- Release the abdominal muscles and allow the breath to flow in.
- Occasionally change the place from which you begin to pull the abdominal muscles in,

for example, begin above the navel or above the pubic arch. However, irrespective of where you begin, pull the whole abdomen in every time. Release the abdominal muscles abruptly and allow the breath to flow in.

- Whilst pulling in the abdominal muscles try, without forcing anything, to lengthen the expiration to about 10 to 15 seconds.
- Limit the incoming breath to a maximum of 5 seconds.
- Avoid drawing breath actively; the incoming breath should be a natural response to releasing the abdominal muscles.
- The abdomen should not be pushed outwards during the incoming breath; the abdomen rises slightly on its own during inspiration.

If you are able to perform the exercises above in a relaxed fashion, you can try to hold your breath for 2 seconds after breathing in and before breathing out. Hold the breath in the entire region of the lowest rib, at both the front, side and back of the body. Never hold the breath in your throat. The lower that you hold the breath in your body, the better.

You now have the rhythm:

- 4 seconds inspiration
- 2 seconds holding the breath low down
- 8 to 10 seconds expiration

When this rhythm goes well, notice that a vacant pause of several seconds naturally arises after the expiration has stopped and before the inspiration begins.

RHYTHMICAL BREATHING

The breathing rhythm is as follows:

- 4 seconds breathing in through the nose
- 3 to 4 seconds holding the breath low in the body
- 10 to 12 seconds pulling in the abdominal muscles and breathing out through the mouth
- 3 to 4 seconds vacant pause

Do the rhythmical breathing every morning for a minimum of 5 minutes, perhaps whilst visualising the colour of the day (see page 21). It is easier to keep your attention on the colour of the day during the breathing than during the performance of the Sun Salutation. In this way you gain optimal effect from both the breathing and the Sun Salutation.

COLOUR AND COLOUR BREATHING

Although we do not realise it the colours that we see daily in our environment, including the colours of the clothes we wear, have a certain influence upon us: sometimes positive and sometimes negative.

Some people wear colourful clothes, others wear black, brown and grey, and yet others always wear the same colour. Then we discover that we react to a certain colour. Such a discovery usually occurs by accident. We feel much nicer in a particular colour or we have a definite aversion to a certain colour. We say 'How can anyone live with such a colour?' At this point colour becomes more important to us; occasionally we stop to reflect and think about it. Or we read in the newspaper that spring depression responds well to light therapy. And think: Yes that is logical. There is so little sun and the weather is constantly grey and overcast. We might then buy a bunch of yellow daffodils to bring a bit of colour into our living room. Thus the first step is taken towards the recognition that colours influence us in certain ways; we treat colours with increased awareness. (Colours emanate from light waves that arise from a special sort of electromagnetic energy and have a wavelength and a vibration frequency). Johannes Itten wrote in his book *Kunst en kleur* (Art and colour): 'Colour is life, colours are the children of the light and the light is the Mother of the colours. Colours are powers of radiation, energies that can affect us in a positive or negative way, whether we are aware of it or not. Colour offers itself to all who wish to use it, but it is only to those who lovingly devote themselves to colours, that it reveals its deeper secrets'.

One of these secrets is colour breathing: using colours to nourish the body via the process of breathing.

The body needs the following colours: red, orange, yellow, green, blue, indigo and violet. It is wonderful if these colours appear in our lives in sufficient quantity. However this is not usually the case and we have to provide for our own colour supply. One possibility is to add the colour of the day during the breathing exercises. This can be done in a variety of ways:

1. We can visualise the colour if we have a

well developed sense of imagery.
2. We can think about the colour, for example a banana for yellow.
3. We can look at coloured paper or cloth and concentrate on the colour.

With each inspiration you breathe the colour in; then breathe out fully; breathe colour in again, and so on. You can use the breathing technique I have described in the chapter on 'Rhythmical breathing' for this.

Use a different colour every day, as shown in the list below, and keep to the colour of the day.

Monday	red
Tuesday	orange
Wednesday	yellow
Thursday	green
Friday	blue
Saturday	indigo
Sunday	violet

Do not mix the colours or only use the colours that appeal to you. Too much of one colour can also disturb the colour balance.

Visualising a colour is not as difficult as you might think. Visualisation is no different than using a thought image. If you think back to something, for example a landscape, beautiful sky or sunset and are able to recall the images by thinking about them, you are also able to visualise.

For some people it can be easier to see a colour before them, if they think for example about fruit: red strawberries, orange oranges, yellow bananas, green apples, etc.

If this still gives problems, use a different piece of material every day. Collect seven pieces of material (or paper) in seven colours. The best is silk; as these colours are very vibrant and bright.

Make sure that the colours are bright:

- bright red instead of dark red
- bright orange instead of dark orange
- bright yellow instead of yellow ochre
- bright green instead of dark green
- bright blue (the colour of the sky on a beautiful summer day)
- indigo: the colour of the night sky studded with stars
- and a dazzling violet

STARTING POSITIONS

When you do the Sun Salutation, the starting position is always important. If the starting position is correct then the effect will be stronger. This also applies to the preparatory exercises.

The right posture also gives the correct muscle tension; in which relaxation is not a slackening of the muscles, but strength in rest. All this combined with good breathing produces an optimal blood circulation and energy flow.

Sitting (on a chair)
For the preparatory exercises in the sitting position it is best to sit on the pelvic floor, legs together, feet on the floor, back straight, crown directed upward and the chin pulled in a little. The tongue is in the middle of the mouth.

Hands

When placing the hands during the Sun Salutation, the pressure and support should lie in the middle of the hands and never through the wrists. You will have to get used to this initially but in the long run it is more comfortable. For most people, taking weight through the wrists is painful and reduces the effectiveness of the exercise. The position in the middle of the hand gives a much better energy effect and strengthens the muscles in the hands, wrists, elbows and shoulders.

Standing

The starting position for the Sun Salutation is standing, with the feet together. If you find this unstable, stand with your feet 10 to 20 cm apart.

The way in which you stand on your feet could also be called: standing in your feet. The better that you contact the ground with your feet, the better the overall muscle tension becomes in the ankles, knees, pelvis, back and neck.

From this position try to feel the following in both feet:

- the left and right side of the forefoot
- relaxed toes (toes not curled up)
- the left and right side of the foot under the ankles
- the heels

Take care:

- not to push the knees too far back
- bottom relaxed, pelvis straight, back straight

- shoulders relaxed
- crown up and chin drawn in
- tongue in the middle of the mouth; the tip of the tongue just above the upper front teeth

In this way you develop a good posture which you can utilize the whole day through when standing. You will notice that you tire less quickly when you stand in a good, active and yet relaxed fashion.

ATTITUDE OF MIND – NECESSARY OR NOT?

During lessons I am often asked 'Can a sportsman or woman use the Sun Salutation simply for physical training or is it essential to incorporate the spiritual background?'

Of course you can make excellent use of the Sun Salutation as physical training. It is a fine exercise irrespective of the sport that you do. The Sun Salutation is a particularly good exercise for sports in which more demand is placed on one side of the body, because the Sun Salutation induces and maintains the correct tension on both sides of the spinal column and pelvis. But the one does not, or does not have to, exclude the other. The Sun Salutation turns into a very different exercise when performed with a little gratitude in the heart.

In the past, the Sun Salutation was a spiritual experience: feeling connected with the Unmentionable from which all things arose; with the Sun as symbol for the giver of life, upon which everything was and continues to be dependent.

The respect for life and the connection with life was considerable, even in daily life, and for many people today is just as real as a thousand years ago. All this was and is expressed in the Sun Salutation.

You stand on the earth which carries and nourishes us. You thank Mother Earth. You consciously experience the air around you and know that you are surrounded by air, you give thanks for this. In this way you thank the rain, wind and moon. Then, with your face to the east, you raise your arms to the sun. You gratefully receive the sunlight with deep peace and reverence in your heart and allow it to penetrate.

In days gone by the Sun Salutation was performed many times in this state of mind. The Sun Salutation can also be done today in this manner. The choice is yours; do you choose to enrich your life or not.

In any case you can give it a try and... who knows, you might even enjoy it.

2

PRELIMINARY

EXERCISES

Not everyone is immediately able to perform the Sun Salutation well or even adequately. Help is required with this, otherwise people tend to give up quickly if movements are difficult to achieve. In my practice I use the preliminary exercises as an aid: initially practising the parts; allowing the body to slowly get used to the different movements. As the body becomes more supple and the muscles gain in strength the transition to the full Sun Salutation becomes feasible.

During the exercises try to breathe well and in particular to breathe out well. A guideline here is: force nothing, neither the movements nor the breathing.

It takes times and attention for your body to become more supple. Time is also needed to allow the changes to occur. Which is why the exercise is also an exercise in patience.

The preliminary exercises are intended to strengthen:

- the arms, wrists and fingers
- the shoulders
- the neck

- the back
- the pelvis
- the knees
- the feet and toes

You can decide for yourself what you need. Some exercises can be carried out in a spare moment, others require more time and space. A few are nice to do under the shower. The exercises that you need to do should be repeated daily.

During and after the exercises try to keep feeling what is happening or what has happened. This is an excellent way of learning to feel your body and to get to know and recognize the reactions of your body.

SPECIFIC NECK AND SHOULDER EXERCISES

An exercise which can be done in a spare moment is the arm circle. This has a beneficial effect on the shoulder capsule and on the ligaments and muscles in the shoulder capsule. If you start early enough with the arm circle the exercise can prevent shoulder complaints due to arthritis in older age.

The arm circle is not initiated from the hand but from the upper arm which actively performs the circular movement. If the arm circle is initiated from the hand, the upper arm is more passive. We need the activity of the upper arm for a good result.

- Lift your right arm up.

- Turn the upper arm backwards.
- Make the circle as big as possible by bringing the upper arm maximally up, back, down and forward.
- Perform the movement a few times in a forward direction.
- Repeat the movement with the left arm.
- Observe the effect.

The next exercises are for getting rid of over tense and painful muscles in the neck and upper back, not of course forgetting the sometimes extremely painful spots between the shoulder blades. These are also exercises that can be done in a spare moment. You can stand or sit for them.

- Sit (or stand) properly.
- Relax your shoulders maximally by pulling them up and then letting them go.
- Pull your shoulders back slowly.
- Keep going and pull both shoulder blades towards each other.
- Hold the tension for a while.
- Release all the tension in one go.
- Repeat this twice and then try to observe what the effect is.

- Relax your shoulders.
- Pull both shoulders up as far as possible.
- Now bring the shoulder blades backwards and press the blades together.
- Hold the tension for a while; your chin will poke out a little.
- First release the tension in your chin and then let the rest of the tension go.

- Repeat twice.
- Observe.

Do not repeat these exercises too often at one time. It is better to repeat them three times, five times a day, than it is to do them fifteen times in one session.

If you have painful muscles you have probably had neck and shoulder problems for some time. The painful feeling can be very pronounced after the exercises; perhaps you think that it has got worse. What it means however is that the muscles are full of waste products which now have to be removed by the blood. This cannot happen in one go; after a while the painful feeling subsides, and returns in a less severe form after the next exercise session. After several weeks of steadfast exercising the muscles become more flexible and the pain disappears.

LEG/FOOT EXERCISES ON A TABLE OR CHAIR

- Sit on your pelvic floor.
- Extend one leg horizontally.
- Allow the extended leg to drop down by relaxing it completely. At the same time extend the other leg.
- Repeat this extending and relaxing ten times and gradually progress to thirty to fifty repetitions.

This strengthens and lubricates the knees.

- Straighten your leg and push the heel as far

away as possible; you can also actively pull your forefoot towards you.
- Alternate this with the other leg.

You can also do this with both legs simultaneously; remember to relax the feet well between the exercises.

- Straighten both legs; form a \ / with the feet by placing the heels together. Simultaneously tense the muscles around the anus and push the heels outwards.
- Repeat this contraction and relaxation of the anus and feet a couple of times.

- Straighten both legs; form a / \ with the feet by placing the big toes together. Tense the bladder and anterior pelvic floor muscles and at the same time push the heels outwards.
- Contract and relax the feet and the bladder and pelvic floor muscles a few times.

- Alternate the exercises above. First, whilst breathing in, bring the big toes together and contract the bladder and anterior pelvic floor muscles.
- Whilst breathing out bring the heels together and tense the anal muscles.
- Repeat this five to ten times.

Sitting on a chair
- Knees and feet together.
- Place the left hand on the outside of the left knee.

- The right hand on the outside of the right knee.
- Try, with anal and bottom muscles tensed, to push your knees outwards whilst resisting this with your hands.
- Relax.
- Repeat this contraction and relaxation five times.

Sitting on a chair
- Feet on the floor about twenty centimetres apart.
- Place the left hand on the inside of the right knee.
- The right hand on the inside of the left knee.
- Try, whilst contracting the bladder and anterior pelvic floor muscles, to push the knees together whilst resisting this with your hands.
- Relax.
- Repeat this contraction five times.

These exercises have a very great effect on the whole body. The exercises strengthen the muscles around the head of the femur, the pelvic floor muscles, the sphincter muscles of the bladder, the muscles around the scrotum of a man and the vaginal muscles of a woman. The arm and shoulder muscles are also strengthened.

PELVIC AND BACK EXERCISES

During the performance of the Sun Salutation the pelvis is the central point that opens and closes with every movement, as often as we repeat the movement. In this way a remarkable circulation is generate in the pelvis which works throughout the body. The stretch over the front of the body is performed from the pelvis and is not difficult. The stretch over the back of the body, from the heel up to and including the bottom, is more difficult and challenging because these muscles are often shortened and it takes time to stretch them. Hence it is important to relax these muscles because only relaxed muscles can lengthen; tense muscles shorten.

- Stand upright.
- Head upright; shoulders relaxed. Place your fingertips over the head of the femur.
- Concentrate on the pelvis.
- Bend forward from the pelvis with a straight back until your upper body is horizontal. The legs remain straight (do not bend or push the knees backward).
- Straighten up again from the pelvis, keeping your back straight.

Feel in particular that you move up and down from this central point. Keep your bottom muscles relaxed. Repeat this several times.

When you can perform the above movement well, move onto the next exercise.

- Head upright.
- Arms hanging loosely by the body.
- Bend forward from the pelvis with a straight back and place your abdomen on your thighs.

- Relax your head, shoulders and arms and allow them to hang down.
- Stay in this position whilst you continue to breathe; the legs remain straight.
- Lift up your head and keeping your back straight return to the upright position via the pelvis.

- Stand upright.
- Spread your arms out sideways.
- Bend forward from the pelvis, keeping your back straight, until your upper body is horizontal. Keep your knees straight.
- Now move twenty centimetres up and down with the arms and from the pelvis.
- Repeat this several times.
- Return to the upright position via the pelvis with your back straight and the head tipped back slightly.

You can repeat this several times but do not force yourself. Try not to push the head too hard against the knees. Remember: tension shortens muscles; relaxation lengthens muscles.

Now you may incorporate the arms.

- Stand upright.
- Arms by the body, the back of the hands facing forward.
- Now focus on the level of your pubic arch

(this area is particularly important in the Sun Salutation).

- Bend over backward from the pubic arch and at the same time lift your arms upwards. At the highest point let your head drop backward (head between the arms).
- Make sure that there is hardly any tension in your back and bottom.
- Breathe in and out gently.
- Lift the head up.
- Now bend forward from the pelvis with a straight back.
- Place your abdomen on your thighs again.
- Relax your head, shoulders and arms.
- Continue to breathe gently.
- Lift up your head and keeping your back straight return to the upright position via the pelvis.

These are the first movements of the Sun Salutation.

Walking with the hands – walking with the feet

The next movement is the step backward which is followed a few movements later by a stride forward which brings the foot between the hands. This movement also needs previous practice.

- Stand upright.
- Bend forward from the pelvis with a straight back.
- Place your abdomen on your thighs.
- Now walk your hands forward across the floor until the body is stretched out. Do

not move your hands too far at any one time, take little steps instead. Keep your heels on the ground for as long as possible. Continue to breathe evenly.

- Walk the hands back over the floor again (use little steps).
- Repeat this a few times.
- Return to the upright position via the pelvis keeping your back straight.

- Stand upright.
- Bend forward from the pelvis with a straight back.
- Place your abdomen on your thighs.
- Put your hands firmly on the floor; take care not to over tense the neck.
- Now walk your feet backward until the body is extended. Use little steps here too; as your body becomes more supple the steps can become longer.

- Keep your heels on the ground for as long as possible during the walking.
- Stay in this extended position with bent toes.
- Continue to breathe gently.
- Then walk the feet back to the hands again.
- Repeat walking back and forth a few times.

During this exercise the knees do not touch the ground.

- Stand upright.
- Take a big step backward with your left leg.
- Now bend your right knee as far as you can. The left leg is stretched out behind you; the top of the foot comes into contact with the ground.
- The upper body remains upright; shoulders and arms relaxed.

- Breathe in and out gently.
- Repeat this with the other leg.

Only when you can perform this well should you go onto the next exercise.

- Stand upright.
- Take a big step backward with your left leg.
- Now bend your right knee; your left knee bends a little too.
- The upper body remains upright; arms and shoulders relaxed.
- Now try from this position to bring the left leg further back with the heel on the ground.
- Make sure that the foot cannot slip away.
- In the outermost position keep breathing gently in and out.
- Repeat this with the other leg.

The next exercise begins in a flexed position; hands alongside or in front of the feet.

- Take a big step backward with your left leg until your toes are on the ground; the head is tipped back a little.
- Continue to breathe evenly.
- Take a big step forward and place the left foot between the hands; the head hangs down in a relaxed way.
- Repeat this with the right leg.

Stand in the flexed position again; hands on the ground.

- Take a big step backwards with your left leg until your leg is stretched and supported by the toes.
- Now bring your right leg back too; the

body is now supported by the hands and feet.

- Now push your bottom up into the air so that your body almost forms a triangle; your head is between your arms.
- Take a big step forwards with the right leg and place the right foot by the hands.
- Do the same with the left foot.
- Breathe evenly throughout the exercise.
- Straighten up again from the pelvis with a straight back.
- Repeat this movement several times, alternating between right and left.

The difficulty with this movement occurs during the step forward: the foot must be placed between the hands again. By placing the foot between the hands, the Sun Salutation acquires a rhythmical progression. If your foot does not get there or only gets halfway, you have to keep moving your hands, which is not ideal for the rhythm or the effectiveness. As the pelvis becomes more supple, the forward step improves. If the step no longer gives you any trouble, the preliminary exercises have done their work and the Sun Salutation itself will be sufficient.

Suspended position

The suspended position is not so difficult to perform well. There are however some points that need attention:

- First practise the half suspended position; then the full.
- The forearms are on the ground in the half suspended position.
- The arms are extended in the full suspended position.
- The shoulders are never pulled up, they stay low.
- As the arms are extended, the pressure lies in the middle of the hand.
- When raising the upper body, the stretch over the front of the body starts from the pelvis, proceeded by the abdomen, midriff and ribcage.
- The head does not tip all the way back.
- The back and bottom muscles are as relaxed as possible during the suspended position; the feet lie straight.
- Make sure that a curve does not appear above the sacrum. If there is a significant curve, then come down immediately. You have used muscle contraction from the back instead of the stretch on the front of the body.

The half suspended position

- Lie on your front. Legs and feet straight; forehead resting on the ground.
- Forearms lie under the shoulders.
- Relax your back and bottom muscles.
- Use the forearms to push the upper body up; the forearms remain on the ground.
- Head with crown upright.

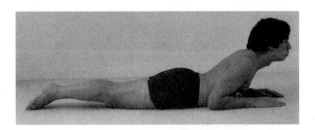

- Feel if your back and bottom muscles are relaxed. You can check this by tensing and then releasing your bottom muscles.
- Keep breathing evenly.
- Return to the starting position and relax.

If your back feels comfortable in this position, then you can do the full suspended position. If however your back is painful or very stiff, you have probably used too much muscle contraction in your back instead of the stretch from the pelvis on the front. In this case do not perform the full suspended position but practise the anterior stretch: pelvis, abdomen, midriff and chest until you notice that your back remains relaxed. The muscle stretching is and remains on the front of the body. If you have had back problems for some time, do not perform the suspended position. Do other back exercises until your back muscles are supple again. The following exercises will do your back good:

- Lie on your back.
- Place a thin cushion under your neck.
- Allow your tongue to lie in the middle of the mouth with the point of the tongue just above the upper front teeth.
- Place your knees on your abdomen. If necessary put your hands on your knees but you must not pull your knees toward the body. Your knees may also hang out sideways on both sides.

Do this for at least five minutes, three times a day, with one of the sessions in the middle of the day. In this way your back muscles remain more relaxed and are better able to carry out their function. Remember: poorly fitting shoes, shoe heels worn down on one side and high heels ruin the back.

The full suspended position

- Lie on your front; legs and feet straight. Forehead resting on the ground.
- The hands lie under the shoulders.
- Relax your back and bottom muscles.
- Push your upper body up from your hands and at the same time bring the body up from the pelvis too.
- Do this slowly, step by step: pelvis, abdomen, midriff and ribcage. Shoulders stay down and slightly back.

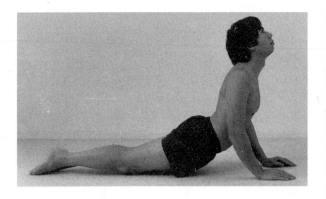

- The head is tipped back a little.
- Feel if your bottom muscles and back are relaxed and try to continue breathing in a relaxed way.
- Come down again, step by step, starting with the head.
- Observe if you can feel changes in your body.

From extended position to undulated position

Adopt the extended position. (The body is supported on hands and toes). Make sure that the back does not sag.

- While you bend your arms, let the body sink towards the ground with the bottom kept up; the abdomen should not touch the ground. The forehead, chest, knees and toes rest on the ground. Continue to breathe gently.
- Push your body into the extended position again.
- Repeat this several times.

Whilst in the extended position and during the up and down movement keep the pressure in the middle of the hands. The tongue lies in the middle of the mouth.

3

THE SIMPLE

SUN SALUTATION

While you faithfully continue to practise those movements that are difficult for you, you may slowly but surely build up to the simple Sun Salutation.

First have a good look at the photographs and then at the succession of the movements. Read and reread the text on the simple Sun Salutation so that you become familiar with it.

Begin with movements 1, 2, 3, and 4 and come back with movements 9, 10 and 1.

If this goes easily and the breathing stays calm, build up the movement further by adding 5 and 6. You then have 1, 2, 3, 4, 5, 6 and then after turning your toes over, return with 9, 10 and 1.

When rhythm has also been achieved in this sequence, 7 and 8 are added and the simple Sun Salutation is complete.

Practise the simple Sun Salutation until the moment comes when your pelvis is literally able to take the big step. Then progress onto the performance of the Sun Salutation.

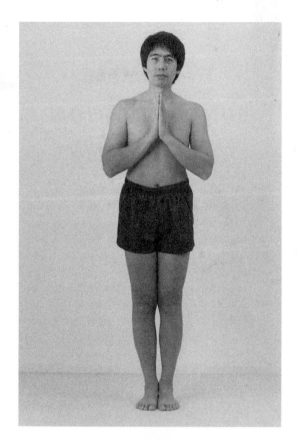

1. Stand upright as described on page 23; palms
    together in front of the chest. Imagine that
    you are standing in the sun and allow the
    warmth of the sun to penetrate.

    The tongue is in the middle of the mouth; the
    tip of the tongue just above the upper front
    teeth.

    Visualize the colour of the day.

    Breathe out by pulling in your abdomen.

2. Whilst you stretch your arms upward (palms uppermost and arms alongside the ears), bend backward from the pelvic arch. Do this whilst breathing in.

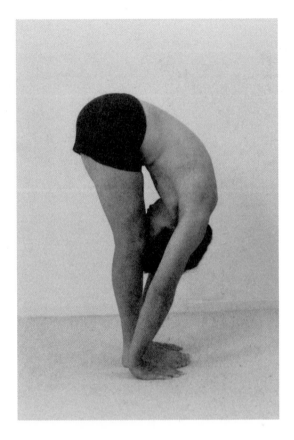

3. Now on an expiration come down, keeping
   the back straight. Place your abdomen on
   your thighs.
   Face directed towards knees; head loose.
   Hands flat on the ground, parallel to the feet.
   Do not push the knees backward.

4. Walk with your hands or feet until you reach the extended position.
   Continue breathing.

5. Bend the arms and allow the body to sink towards the ground. The abdomen must not touch the ground. The forehead, chest, knees and toes do however rest on the ground. Breathe in.

6. Whilst you extend the arms and the
   abdomen touches the ground, place the
   upper side of the toes flat on the ground.
   Now bend the body backward. The pelvis
   stays on the ground, the back is relaxed. The
   stretch is on the front of the body.
   The head not too far back.
   Breathe out.

7. Place the feet on the toes again. Push and lift up the pelvis using the arms, toes and pelvis. Breathe in.

8. In this inverted position, push the heels in the direction of the ground.
The head is between the arms.
Breathe out.

9. Walk with your hands or feet until the hands are alongside the feet.

10. Come up into standing with a straight back.
    Breathe in and finish with 1.

If you want to do one or more sequences, go on by bending over backwards.

It is intended that the inspiration be short and the expiration somewhat longer. You can perform the expiration by actively pulling in your abdominal muscles.

As, in the course of time, the respiration becomes stronger, the body regulates the rhythm of the movements, inspiration and expiration itself.

4

THE SUN

SALUTATION

A FEW GUIDELINES FOR THE PERFORMANCE OF THE SUN SALUTATION

- Use a well ventilated room.
- Wear as little clothing as possible.
- In the winter however, wear socks and perhaps a T-shirt.
- Put a rug or towel on the floor.
- Empty your bowels and bladder before you begin.
- Do not eat anything beforehand.
- First drink a glass of tepid water. This has a beneficial effect on the digestive and excretory organs.
- The tongue lies flat in the mouth. The tip of the tongue is just above the upper front teeth.
- Let go of everything that is bothering you.
- Make space for a pleasant feeling; let this feeling expand.
- As you begin, first think about the sun and allow it to shine on your body and warm you.
- Select the colour of the day and breathe it

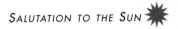
in and out during the Sun Salutation.
- Do not retain the borders of the body in a constrained way.
- Allow that the borders of the body become vague and spacious.

BREATHING DURING THE PERFORMANCE OF THE SUN SALUTATION

If you have learnt to perform the breathing exercises well, you will be able to control all your abdominal muscles. It should now be really easy to pull in the abdominal muscles fairly strongly in one go. This strong abdominal contraction occurs in the Sun Salutation during an expiratory movement, in order to allow inspiration to follow with an inspiratory movement. Thus not actively drawing in breath, but allowing the inspiration to flow inwards. This passive inward flow is a logical effect of releasing the abdominal muscles after expiration. Hence pull in abdomen, breathe out. After releasing the abdominal muscles, the inspiration follows spontaneously.

In the beginning you can follow the breathing recommended for each movement; the tempo is usually on the slow side. But a time will come when you no longer find this comfortable; your tempo has speeded up. Your stamina has improved considerably and your breathing is stronger. The time has now come to allow the body to regulate its own rhythm for breathing and moving. This takes a bit of getting used to in the beginning. The fact that the body can regulate this itself requires trust and surrender. This applies to all types of physical training. Remember that sprinters, joggers, rowers, skaters and other sportsmen and women do not regulate their breathing themselves.

If a top sportsman has a gold medal day then things are going exceptionally well: his body has as it were grown wings and exceeded everything thought possible until that time. The respiration has become an instrument that plays itself.

Then comes the wish to repeat that magical moment, but this is impossible; you cannot go back in time. What you can do at a certain moment however, is to BE there full of trust and surrender again. Just like the Norwegian skater, Koss was in every competition; his body reached previously unknown levels of achievement, thanks to his trust and surrender.

Although the performance of the Sun Salutation and a top competition are hardly comparable, they do have something in common: the opportunity to experience that the body is capable of many things provided you do not regulate it.

THE SUN SALUTATION

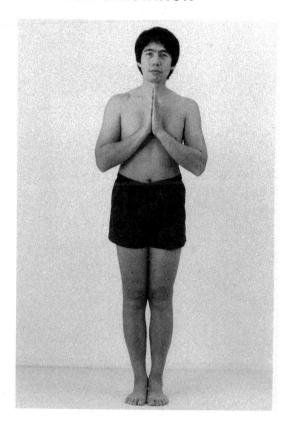

1. Stand upright as described on page 23; palms together in front of the chest. Imagine that you are standing in the sun and allow the warmth to penetrate. The tongue is in the middle of the mouth; the tip of the tongue just above the upper front teeth.
Now visualise the colour of the day.
Breathe out by pulling in your abdomen.

2. Whilst you stretch your arms upwards (palms uppermost and arms next to the ears) bend backwards from the pubic arch. Do this with an inspiration.

3. Now come down on an expiration, keeping
the back straight. Place the abdomen as it
were on your thighs.
The face directed towards the knees; the
head loose.

4. On an inspiration, bring the right leg backwards using a large step; toes and knee on the ground. The head tipped back slightly.

5. Now bring the left leg backwards. The head,
   back and legs form a straight line.
   Breathe out in this extended position.

6. Bend the arms and allow the body to sink towards the ground. The abdomen should not touch the ground. The forehead, knees and toes rest on the ground.
    Breathe in.

7. While you extend your arms and the
   abdomen touches the ground, place the
   upper side of the toes flat on the ground.
   Now bend the body backwards. The pelvis
   stays on the ground, the back is relaxed. The
   stretch occurs over the front of the body.
   The head is not too far back.
   Breathe out.

8. Place the feet on the toes again. Push and lift up the pelvis using the arms, toes and pelvis. Breathe in.

9. In this inverted position, push the heel in the direction of the ground. The head is between the arms.
   Breathe out.

10. Now bring the right leg forwards using a big
    step and place the foot between the hands.
    Breathe in.

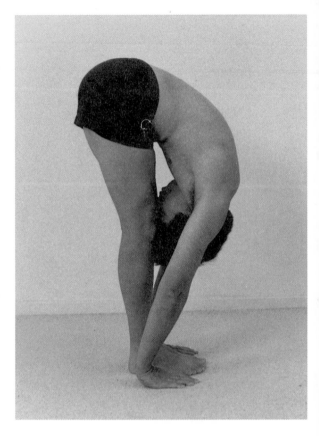

11. Now do the same with the left leg. The feet
    are next to each other, the hands next to the
    feet.
    Bottom in the air; head facing the knees.
    Breathe out.

12. Come up into standing with a straight back;
    arms next to the ears.
    Breathe in.

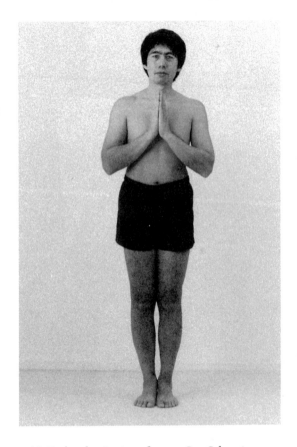

13. End or beginning of a new Sun Salutation.

If you want to do more sequences, go on by bending backwards.

It is intended that the inspiration is short and the expiration slightly longer. You can expire by pulling in the abdominal muscles actively. If, after a time, the breathing becomes strong, the body regulates the rhythm of the movements, inspiration and expiration itself.

THE SUN PRAYER OF
THE SIOUX INDIANS

'Great Spirit, whose voice I know in the wind
and whose Breath brings Life to the world,
listen to me.

I enter into Your presence as one of Your many
children. I am small and weak, I need Your
strength and wisdom.

Allow me to roam in Beauty and let my eyes for-
ever see the purple-red sunset.

May my hands honour the things You have cre-
ated, and my ears hear Your voice.

Make me wise, so that I can understand
the things You have taught my people, the
knowledge which You have hidden in every
leaf and every rock.

I long for strength, not to have power over my
brothers, but to fight against my greatest
enemy, my ego.

Grant that I am always ready to meet You, with
untainted hands and honest eyes, so that my
spirit can come to You without being
ashamed when Life disappears like the setting Sun'.

Rita Beintema